The new word

68210

155·3
DEB

ISBN 0 7062 3326 3
Design David Roberts
Printed in Spain for
Ward Lock Educational, 116 Baker Street, London W1M 2BB

Understanding the nature of lateral thinking and the need for it is the first step towards using it. But understanding and goodwill are not enough. The formal routines suggested as methods of applying lateral thinking are more practical but there is a great need for something more definite, more simple, and more universal. Some tool for applying lateral thinking just as NO is a tool for applying logical thinking.

NO **and** PO

The concept of logical thinking is selection and this is brought about by the processes of acceptance and rejection. Rejection is the basis of logical thinking. The rejection process is incorporated in the concept of the negative. The negative is a judgment device. It is the means whereby one rejects certain arrangements of information. The negative is used to carry out judgment and to indicate rejection. The concept of the negative is crystallized into a definite language tool. This language tool consists of the words no and not. Once one learns the function and use of these words one has learned how to use logical thinking. The whole concept of logical thinking is concentrated in the use of this language tool. Logic could be said to be the management of NO.

The concept of lateral thinking is insight restructuring and this is brought about through the rearrangement of information. Rearrangement is the basis of lateral thinking and rearrangement means escape from the rigid patterns established by experience. The rearrangement process is incorporated in the concept of the (re) laxative. The laxative is a rearranging device. It is the means whereby one can escape from established patterns and create new ones. The laxative allows the arrangement of information in new ways from which new patterns can arise. The concept of the laxative is crystallized into a definite language tool. This language tool is PO. Once one learns the function and use of PO one has learned how to use lateral thinking. The whole concept of lateral thinking is concentrated in the use of this language tool. Lateral thinking could be said to be the management of PO just as logical thinking is the management of NO.

PO is to lateral thinking what NO is to logical thinking. NO is a rejection tool. PO is an insight restructuring tool. The concept of the laxative is the basis of lateral thinking just as the concept of the negative is the basis of logical thinking. Both concepts have to be crystallized into language devices. It is essential to have language devices because of the passive nature of the mechanism of mind. The language devices are themselves patterns which interact with other patterns on the self-organizing memory surface of mind to bring about certain effects. Such language devices are extremely useful in one's own thinking and for communication they are essential.

Although both NO and PO function as language tools the operations they carry out are totally different. NO is a judgment device. PO is an antijudgment device. NO works within the framework of reason. PO works outside that framework. PO may be used to produce arrangements of information that are unreasonable but they are not really unreasonable because lateral thinking functions in a different way from vertical thinking. Lateral thinking is not irrational but arational. Lateral thinking deals with the patterning of information not with the judgement of those patterns. Lateral thinking is prereason. PO is never a judgment device. PO is a construction device. PO is a patterning device. The patterning process may also involve depatterning and repatterning.

Although PO is a language tool it is at the same time an antilanguage device. Words themselves are just as much cliché patterns as the way they are put together. PO provides a temporary escape from the discrete and ordered stability of language which reflects the established patterns of a self-organizing memory system. That is why the full function of PO is unlikely to have evolved in the development of language. Instead PO arises from consideration of the patterning behaviour of the mind.

The function of PO is the rearrangement of information to create new patterns and to restructure old ones. These two functions are but different aspects of the same process but for convenience they may be separated.

● Creating new patterns.
● Challenging old patterns.
  These two functions can be expressed in another way:
● Provocative and permissive: putting information together in new ways and allowing unjustified arrangements of information.
● Liberating: disrupting old patterns in order to allow the imprisoned information to come together in a new way.

The first function of PO: creating new arrangements of information

Experience arranges things in patterns. Things in the environment may happen to be arranged in a particular pattern or else attention may pick things out in a certain pattern. In one case the pattern is derived from the environment and in the other case it is derived from the memory surface of mind since this directs attention. The first function of PO is to create arrangements of information that do not arise from either of these two sources. Just as NO is used to weaken arrangements that are based on experience so PO is used to generate connections that have nothing to do with experience.

Once information has 'settled' into fixed patterns on the
memory surface* then new arrangements can only
occur if they are directly derived from these patterns.
Only such trial arrangements of information are
allowed as would be consistent with these background
patterns. Anything else is dismissed at once. Yet if
(somehow) different arrangements of information
could be brought about and held for a short while then
the information might snap together to form a new
pattern that was either consistent with the background
pattern or capable of altering it. This process is shown
diagrammatically opposite. The purpose of PO is then
either to bring about arrangements that would
otherwise not occur or to protect from dismissal
arrangements that would otherwise be dismissed as
impossible. These functions may be listed as follows:

- To arrange information in a way which would never
  have come about in the normal course of events.
- To hold an arrangement of information without
  judging it.
- To protect from dismissal an arrangement of
  information which has already been judged as impossible.

An arrangement of information is usually judged as
soon as it comes about. The judgment results in one of
two verdicts: 'This is permissible', or 'This is not
permissible'. The arrangement is either affirmed or
denied. There is no middle course. The function of PO
is to introduce a middle course as suggested in the
diagram. PO is never a judgment. It does not quarrel with
the verdict but with the very application of the
judgment. PO is an antijudgment device.

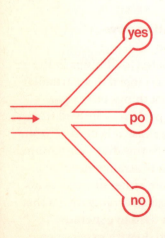

PO allows one to hold an arrangement for a little longer
without having to affirm or deny it. PO delays judgment.

The usefulness of delaying judgment is one of the most
basic principles of lateral thinking. It is also one of the

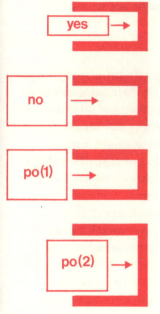

fundamental points of difference from vertical thinking. With vertical thinking an arrangement of information must be right at every step, which means that one must use judgment at the earliest possible opportunity. With lateral thinking an arrangement of information may be wrong in itself but can lead to a perfectly valid new idea. This possibility arises directly from consideration of the mind as a self-maximizing memory surface.

By delaying judgment and holding onto an idea a number of things may happen. If the idea is pursued far enough it may be found to make sense. If one holds onto the idea then freshly arrived information can interact with the idea to give a valid idea. The unjudged idea may direct the search for information that can prove useful in its own right. Finally if the idea is held long enough then the context into which it did not fit may itself be changed.

Exactly the same considerations apply to the use of PO for protection of arrangements of information that have already been judged and dismissed. Such dismissed arrangements may have been dismissed long ago and it may be a matter of resurrecting them under the protection of PO. On the other hand the arrangements may have been proposed and dismissed only recently.

It is important to realize that the use of PO for creating new arrangements of information is quite different from the use of the usual devices for arranging information.

- PO does not have an addition function as provided by 'and'.
- PO does not have an identity function as provided by 'is'.
- PO does not have an alternative function as provided by 'or'.

The function of PO *is to bring about a provocative*

arrangement of information without saying anything at all about it. The arrangement itself is not important but what happens next is. The purpose of the arrangement is to lead forward to new ideas.

In practice there are certain specific occasions on which it is convenient to use PO.

● Juxtaposition
The simplest use of PO is to hold two unrelated things together in order to allow them or their associations to interact. No connection or relationship at all is implied between the two things. Nor is there any reason for putting them together (except what might happen). Without the PO device one would not easily be able to put things together in this way without finding, suggesting, or forcing some reason.
One might say, 'computers PO omelettes'.
From this juxtaposition might come such ideas as:
Cooking by computer or by some preset automatic device. Another idea would be a central store of recipes and one would use a telephone to dial in your ingredients and requirements in order to be given a matched recipe. Both omelettes and computers are concerned with the changing of raw material into a more usable form. In an omelette things are mixed up but come out in a definite form so with a certain type of computer an apparently random mixing of information would still result in some definite output (as for instance in the brain).

● Introduction of a random word
Instead of linking two unconnected words together as in juxtaposition PO can be used to 'introduce' a random unconnected word into a discussion in order to stimulate new ideas. You could say, 'Gentlemen you know all about lateral thinking and the use of a random input to help disturb cliché patterns of thought and to

stimulate new ideas. I am now going to introduce such a random word. This word has no connection at all with what we have been discussing. There is no reason behind my choice of the word. The only reason for its use is the hope that it will provoke some new ideas. Do not feel that there really is a hidden reason. Do not spend your time searching for this reason. The word is 'raisin'. Instead of saying all that one would simply say: 'Po raisin'.

If the problem under discussion was, 'How to use study time' then this random word could set off such ideas as: raisin—used to make cakes enjoyable—small pockets of sweetness—intersperse short periods of more interesting subjects among longer periods of less interesting subjects —create small nodes of interest in less interesting subjects.

raisins—dried grapes—concentrated sweetness— concentrate and summarize material so that it can be taken in over a shorter time.

raisins—exposed in the sun to dry—perhaps one can study in a pleasant surrounding as easily as in an unpleasant one—does lighting, colour etc affect boredom. Perhaps material can be subjected to 'glare' of analysis by someone else in order to reduce it to its essentials.

raisins—dried for preservation—notes and summaries easier to remember but need reconstituting with fluid (i.e. examples).

● Disconnected jumps
In vertical thinking one moves in sequential steps but in lateral thinking one can make disconnected jumps and then try and fill in the gaps. If you do this in the middle of a vertical thinking discussion then everyone else will be very confused as they try to find the logic behind this jump. In order to indicate that the jump is a lateral disconnected one you could preface your comment

with PO. For instance in the discussion about study time you might say, 'Po time spent studying is time spent not doing other things'.

The jump may be only a small one within the same field or it may be a large one to an unconnected field. PO saves one the trouble of having to link the new remark to what has gone before. As usual PO implies, 'Don't look for the reason behind this. Let us just go forward and see what the *effect* of it is.'

● Doubt (semi-certainty)
Whenever a discussion gets blocked by the impossibility of proving a certain point PO can be used to open things up again. PO does not prove the point or deny it but it allows the point to be used in any way which will enable the discussion to keep going. One can then see what happens. It may be that nothing very useful comes of it and one realizes that the original point was not so vital after all. It may be that one can reach a solution and from this one can find another way back to the starting point without having to go through the doubtful point. It may be that one can only reach a solution through the doubtful point and so one comes to realize how vital this point is and therefore increases the effort to prove it. This particular use of PO is not very different from the ordinary use of 'if' or 'suppose'.

● Being wrong
In lateral thinking one does not mind being wrong on the way to a solution because it may be necessary to go through a wrong area in order to get to a position from which the correct path is visible. PO is an escort that allows one to move through the wrong area. PO does not make things right but it switches attention from why something is wrong to how it may be useful. In effect PO implies, 'I know this is wrong but I am going to put things this way in order to see where it leads me'.

In considering the problem of keeping the windscreen of a car free from dirt and water someone suggested that cars ought to be driven backward since the back window was always much easier to see out of than the front window. In itself this is obviously nonsense since if one was going backwards that window would get just as dirty as the ordinary windscreen. Nevertheless the suggestion, 'Why not drive backwards' can lead on to such other ideas as indirect vision systems or some way of protecting the windscreen from head on exposure to mud and water.

In this example PO would be used in the following way. Someone would suggest driving backwards and this would be met with the response, 'That's nonsense, because . . . . ' The reply to this would be, 'Po why not drive backwards'. The purpose of PO would be to delay judgment – to hold the idea in mind for a few moments in order to see what could arise from it instead of dismissing it at once.

● Holding function
In addition to protecting an idea which is obviously wrong PO can be used to protect an idea from judgment. In this case the idea has not already been judged but is about to be subjected to critical analysis. PO is used to *delay* this. This function of PO is rather similar to its use for the introduction of a random stimulus. An ordinary remark or idea in the course of a discussion is turned by the use of PO into a catalyst. Used in such circumstances PO indicates: 'Let's not bother to analyse whether this is right or wrong – let us just see what ideas it will lead to.'

PO could be used by the person offering the idea or it could be used by anyone else. Thus if an evaluation of the idea was started someone could simply interject, 'Po . . . . ' This would mean, 'Let's hold off evaluation for the moment'.

● Construction

In school geometry a problem is often made easier to solve by adding some additional lines to the original figure. This process is similar to that involved in the story of the lawyer whose task it was to divide up eleven horses among three sons so that one of them got half of the horses, another got a quarter, and the third son got one sixth. What he did was to lend his own horse to the sons and then divided the twelve horses up, giving the first son six, the second three and the third two. He then took his own horse back again.

Here PO is used to add something to the problem or to change it in some other way. Changing the problem in this way can lead to new lines of development, new ways of looking at it. The purpose of changing the problem is *not* to rephrase it or put it in a better way but to alter it and see what happens next. For instance in considering the efficiency of the police in dealing with crime one might say, 'Po why not employ one-armed policemen?' Changing the problem in this way by adding the factor of 'one-armed policemen' would focus attention on the possible advantages of being one-armed and especially on the need to use brain and organization rather than muscle power.

Summary

There are many other ways in which PO can be used but the occasions listed above are enough to illustrate the *first* function of PO. This first function is quite simply to allow one to say anything one likes. PO allows one to arrange information in any way whatsoever. There need be no justification at all for such arrangement except PO.

Po two and two make five.
Po water flows uphill if it is coloured green.
Po lateral thinking is a waste of time.
Po men have souls and women have not.

Po it takes a lifetime to unlearn what has been learned in education.

The first function of PO is to shift attention from the meaning of a statement and the reason for making it to the effect of the statement. With PO one looks forwards instead of backward. Because any arrangement of information can lead on to other arrangements a statement can be very useful as a stimulus no matter how nonsensical it is in itself. And by being nonsensical one can arrange information in a way that is different from the established patterns – and so increase the chance of a permanent restructuring. With vertical thinking one is not allowed to do any of this. With vertical thinking one looks backwards at the reason for a statement, at the justification, at the meaning.

The statement, 'Po water flows uphill if it is coloured green' is ridiculous but it could lead on to such ideas as: Why should the green colour make a difference? Why should adding colour make a difference? Is there anything one could add to water to make it flow uphill? In fact there is. If one adds a very small amount of a special plastic then the water acts as a solid/liquid to such an extent that if you start pouring water out of a jug and then hold the jug upright the water will continue to siphon out, climbing up the side of the jug, flowing over the rim and down the outer side.

PO as a device allows one to use information in this way which is completely different from the ordinary use of information. One could use information in this way without PO but one would still be using the lateral concept which is incorporated in PO. The convenience of PO as an actual language device is that it clearly indicates that information is being used in this special way. Without such an indication there would be confusion as the listener would not know what was going on. A PO type statement inserted into an ordinary vertical thinking discussion without the use of PO would lead the listeners to suppose that the speaker was mad, lying, mistaken, stupid, ignorant or facetious. Apart from the inconvenience of being the recipient of such judgments there is the danger of being taken seriously. For instance, 'Po the house is on fire' is rather different from 'The house is on fire'. Furthermore if one does not use PO then the information is not used as a stimulus in the lateral manner.

The second function of PO: challenging old arrangements of information

The basic function of mind is to create patterns. The memory surface of mind organizes information into patterns. Or rather it allows information to organize itself into patterns.* The effect is just the same as if the mind picked things out of the environment and put them together to give patterns. Once formed these patterns become ever more firmly established because they direct attention. The effectiveness of mind depends entirely on the creation, the recognition and the use of patterns. The patterns have to be permanent to be of any use. Yet the patterns are not necessarily the only way of putting together the information contained in them—or even the best. The patterns are determined by the time of arrival of the information or by preceding patterns that have been accepted entire.

The second function of PO is to challenge these established patterns. PO is used as a freeing device to free one from the fixity of established ideas, labels, divisions, categories and classifications. The way PO is used can be summarized under the following headings:

● To challenge the arrogance of established patterns.
● To question the validity of established patterns.
● To disrupt established patterns and liberate

information that can come together to give new patterns.
- To rescue information trapped by the pigeonholes of labels and classifications.
- To encourage the search for alternative arrangements of the information.

- Never a judgment
  As suggested before PO is never used as a judgment device. PO is never used to indicate whether an arrangement of information is right or wrong. PO is never used to indicate whether an arrangement of information is likely or unlikely or whether it is the best available at the moment. PO is a device to bring about an arrangement or rearrangement of information not a device to judge the new arrangements or condemn the old ones.

  PO implies, 'That may be the best way of looking at things or putting the information together. That may even turn out to be the only way. But let us look around for other ways.'

  With vertical thinking one is not allowed to challenge an idea unless one can show why it is wrong or else provide an alternative. If one provides an alternative one must somehow show why this alternative is preferable to the original idea as well as proving that the alternative is sound. With PO one has to do none of these things. One challenges the established order without necessarily being able to offer anything in its place or even to show any deficiency.

  Judgment usually asks for justification of an idea. Justification of why an arrangement of information should be accepted. One wants to know why something has been put together in a certain way. With PO the emphasis is shifted away from this 'why' to 'where to'. One accepts the need to rearrange information in new

ways. One takes a new arrangement and instead of
trying to see where it has come from and whether it is
justified one sees where it leads to—*what effect it can
have.*

● The response to PO
The challenge of PO is not met by a fierce defence of
why the established idea is indeed the best possible
way of putting things together because PO does not
attack an idea. PO is a challenge to try and think of
other ways. The challenge of PO is met by generating
different ways of looking at the situation. The more
ways one can generate the more clearly it may be shown
that the original idea was indeed the best one but that
is no reason for refusing to try and generate other ways.
If in generating these alternative ways a new and
better way of looking at things turns up then that can
only be a good thing. Even if the old idea is only
altered slightly that is still a good thing. Even the
possibility that there might be another way of looking
at things is useful in itself in so far as it lessens the
rigidity of the old idea and makes it more easily changed
when change is due.

● Challenging cliché patterns
Any pattern that is at all useful is a cliché. The more
useful it is the more of a cliché it tends to become.
And the more of a cliché it is the more useful it may
become. PO can be used to challenge any cliché. PO
not only challenges the way concepts are arranged into
patterns but the very concepts themselves. One always
tends to think of clichés as arrangements of concepts
but that the concepts themselves must be accepted as
the building blocks of thought and so must themselves
remain unaltered.

'Po freedom' challenges the very concept of freedom
not the value or purpose of freedom.

'Po punishment' challenges the very concept of punishment not the circumstances under which it is used or the purpose for which it is used.

As suggested above it is the useful concepts that need challenging most. The less useful concepts are likely to be under perpetual challenge and reformation. But the usefulness of a useful concept protects it.

● Focusing
Since the cliché may refer to a particular concept or a phrase or to the whole idea it is helpful if one is specific about what is being challenged by PO. In order to do this one would repeat what is being challenged but preface it with PO.

'It is the function of education to train the mind and to pass on to it the knowledge of ages.'

To this one might reply: 'Po, train the mind' or 'Po the knowledge of ages', or even just 'Po train'.

Used in this way PO can act as a *focusing* device to direct attention to some concept that is always taken for granted because there are other concepts which seem more open to reexamination.

● Alternatives
There are times when it is reasonable to try and find other ways of looking at a situation. This happens when the current approach is not satisfactory. PO is used as a demand to generate alternatives even when it is quite *unreasonable*. One goes on generating alternatives right up to the point of absurdity – and beyond. Since there is no good reason for generating alternatives under these circumstances one needs the artificial stimulus of PO which is a device that works outside of reason.
'It is spring and the bird is on the wing.'

'No. The wing is on the bird.'
'Po'
'The bird and the wing both happen to be going along in the same direction.'

Used in this way PO is an invitation (or a demand) to generate alternative arrangements of the information. It is also used to justify those alternative arrangements by making it clear that they are offered as alternative arrangements and not necessarily better arrangements or even justified ones.

● Antiarrogance
One of the most valuable functions of PO is as an antiarrogance device. PO is a reminder of the behaviour of the memory surface of mind. PO is a reminder that a particular arrangement of information which seems inevitable may yet have come about in an arbitrary fashion. PO is a reminder that the illusion of certainty may be useful but that it cannot be absolute. PO is a reminder that certainty about a particular arrangement of information can never exclude the possibility of there being another arrangement. PO challenges dogmatism and absolutism. PO challenges the arrogance of any absolute statement or judgment or point of view.

Used in this way PO does not imply that the statement is wrong. It does not even imply that the person using PO has doubts about the statement let alone justified doubts. All PO implies is that the statement is being made with a degree of arrogance that is not justified under any circumstances.

PO implies the following: 'You may be right and your logic may be faultless. Nevertheless you are starting from perceptions that are arbitrary and you are using concepts that are arbitrary since both are derived from your own individual experience or the general experience of a particular "culture". There are also the limitations of the information processing system of mind. You may be right within a particular context or using particular concepts but these are not absolute.'

PO used in this fashion is never intended to introduce so much doubt that an idea becomes unusable. PO is never directed at an idea itself but only at the arrogance surrounding it—at the exclusion of other possibilities.

● Counteracting NO
NO is a very convenient device for handling information. It is a very definite and a very absolute device. NO also tends to be a permanent label. The permanence of the label, its definiteness and its absolute rejection, may rest on evidence that was at best flimsy. Once the label is applied however then the full force of the label takes over and the bare adequacy of the reason behind its application is lost. It may also happen that the label was justified when it was originally applied but that things have changed and the label is now no longer justified. Unfortunately the label remains until it is removed—it does not only last so long as there are reasons for it to last. Nor is it easy to examine whether there are sufficient reasons for maintaining the label because one cannot know whether a label is worth reexamining until one has in fact done so and the NO label itself deters such examination.

PO is used to counteract the absolute block caused by the NO label. As usual PO is not a judgment. PO does not imply that the NO label is incorrect nor does it even suggest that there is doubt about the label. In effect PO implies: 'Let us cover up that NO label for the moment and proceed as if it was not there.' As one goes forward with one's examination it may become obvious that the label is no longer justified. On the other hand it may become obvious that the label is still as valid as ever but nevertheless information which has been hidden behind the label may be very useful elsewhere.

Consider the statement: 'You cannot live if your heart stops.' This would be changed to 'Po you can live if your heart stops' and this leads on to consideration of the artificial devices for keeping a heart beating, for artificial hearts or transplanted hearts. It also leads on to the need for a new criterion of death since the heart can be kept beating by artificial means even when the brain is irreversibly damaged.

The history of science is full of instances when something was said not to be possible but later proved to be possible. Heavier than air flying machines are an example. In 1941 someone showed that to get a load weighing one pound to the moon would require a rocket weighing one million tons. Eventually the rocket that actually sent men to the moon weighed far less.

Any definite use of the NO label is an invitation to use PO.

● Antidivision
In so far as PO is used to challenge concepts it also challenges the division which divides something into two separate concepts. PO challenges not only the concepts but the division that has brought them about. The pattern making tendency of mind can both put together things that ought to be separated and also separate things that ought to be put together. Both an artificial difference and an artificial sameness may be challenged with PO.

If two things are separated by a division then PO may

challenge the division or may shift attention towards the features which the two things have in common and away from those features that separate them.

Rigid divisions, classifications, categories and polarizations all have a great usefulness but they can also be limiting. As with NO the function of PO is to temporarily lift the labels and let the information come together again for reassessment. Information is dragged out of pigeonholes and allowed to interact. Things may be classified by a particular feature or by a particular function. Once classified the label becomes permanent and as a result all the other features and functions tend to be forgotten. One does not think of looking under a label for a function that is not indicated on that label. As in a filing system something is more effectively lost if it is misfiled than if it is not filed at all.

A spade and a broom are two very different things. 'Spade po broom' focuses attention on the similarities: in both a function is performed at the end of a shaft, both have long shafts, both can be used in a right-handed or a left-handed manner, in both there is a wide part at the end of the narrow part, both can be used for removing material from a place, both could be used as a weapon, both could be used to prop a door open etc.

'Artist po technologist.' One is very ready to put people into pigeonholes and the further the pigeonholes are apart the more useful they seem to be. They seem to be more useful because with far apart pigeonholes one finds it easier to predict what a person is going to do than if the pigeonholes overlapped. 'Artist po technologist' challenges the big gap there is supposed to be between the two types. It suggests that the two types may be both trying to do the same thing: to achieve an effect. The materials may be different but the methods may be the same: a combination of experience, information, experimentation and judgment. It may also suggest that nowadays an artist has to be something of a technologist if he is to use the newer media.

● Diversion

PO challenges concepts, it challenges the division between concepts, and it can also be used to challenge the line of development of a concept. Sometimes the line of development of an idea is so natural and so obvious that one moves quite smoothly along this path before ever wondering whether there might be an alternative path to be explored. To prevent this PO may be used as a temporary blocking device. PO is used as a special sort of NO but without the judgment of NO or the permanence of NO. In effect PO implies: 'That is the natural path of development but we are going to block that path for the moment in order to make it possible to explore some other pathways.'

'A business exists to make profits. Profits are obtained from the most efficient methods of production coupled with thorough marketing and the maximum price the market will bear . . . .' This is a natural and reasonable line of thought. But if one were to challenge, 'Po to make profits' then one would be able to explore other possible developments. 'A business has the social function of providing an environment in which people can make the maximum contribution to society through productivity.'
'A business exists as an efficient production unit. Efficiency is the main aim not profit.'
'A business only exists as an evolutionary stage in the organization of production and its only justification is historical.'

If PO is used skillfully it can divert the line of thought into new pathways by blocking the old ones at certain crucial points. PO is an excuse for choosing a line of thought that is not the most obvious or the best.

● PO and overreaction
The general function of PO is as a laxative to relax the rigidity of a particular way of looking at things. In certain situations a rigid way of looking at things can lead to emotional overreaction. In such cases PO acts as a laugh or a smile to release the tension that accompanies a rigid point of view. Both a laugh and a smile occur when a particular way of looking at a situation is suddenly turned around. PO suggests the possibility of such a change in view. PO acts to lessen the fierce necessity of a particular point of view.

General function of PO

PO is the laxative of language and thinking. PO is the device for carrying out lateral thinking.

PO is a symbol which draws attention to the pattern making behaviour of mind which tends to establish rigid patterns. PO draws attention to the possibility of clichés and rigid ways of looking at things. PO draws attention to the possibility of insight restructuring to obtain new patterns without any further information. Even if PO is never used except as a reminder of these things then it can still be extremely useful.

When used as a practical language tool the function of PO is to indicate that lateral thinking is being used. PO indicates that the arrangement of information being made makes sense from a lateral thinking point of view even if it does not make sense otherwise. Without some definite indicator such as PO there would be confusion when lateral thinking was introduced in the middle of an ordinary vertical thinking discussion.

PO is not a selective device but a generative one. PO is

never a judgment. PO never examines why an arrangement of information has been made but looks forward to what effect it may have. PO does not oppose or counteract judgments but merely sidesteps them. PO also protects arrangements of information from judgment.

PO is essentially a device to enable one to use information in a way that is other than the most obvious and the most reasonable. PO allows one to make arrangements of information for which there is no justification. PO also allows one to challenge arrangements of information for which there is full justification.

PO may seem a perversion designed to upset the highly useful system of logical thinking, permanent concepts and the pursuit of the most obvious. PO is not however a perversion but an escape. It does not destroy the usefulness of this system but adds to it by overcoming the rigidity which is the main limitation of the system. It is a *holiday* from the usual conventions of logic not an attack upon them. Without the stabilizing background of traditional vertical thinking PO would not be much use. If everything was chaos then there would be no rigidity to escape from nor would there be any possibility of establishing a more up to date pattern which is what insight is about. As a device PO actually enhances the effectiveness of vertical thinking by keeping it intact. This PO does by providing a means to bypass vertical thinking in order to introduce a generative factor. Once a new pattern has emerged it can be developed with the full rigour of vertical thinking and judged.

Similarity of PO to other words
It may be felt that some of the functions of PO are very similar to those carried out by such words as hypothesis, possible, suppose and poetry. There are some functions

of PO which are indeed similar for instance the semicertainty function. But there are other functions of PO which are quite different for instance the juxtaposition of totally unrelated material. Hypothesis, possible and suppose are very weak relations of PO. They cover arrangements of information which seem very reasonable but cannot quite be proved. They are tolerable guesses at the best arrangement of information at the moment. PO in contrast allows information to be used in ways which are *totally* unreasonable. The most important difference is that with these words the information is used for its own sake even if the use is tentative. With PO however the information is not used for its own sake but for its effect. Perhaps the most similar word is poetry where words are used not so much for their own meaning as for their stimulating effect.

The mechanism of PO

Why should PO work? PO could never work in a linear system like a computer because the arrangement of information in such a system is always the best possible one according to the programme. But in a self-maximizing system or a system with humour the arrangement of information into patterns depends very heavily on the sequence of arrival of information. Thus A followed by B, followed by C, followed by D, would give a different pattern to B followed by D, followed by A, followed by C. But if A, B, C and D were all to arrive together then the best arrangement of them would be different from either of the other two arrangements. There is a tremendous continuity in this type of system and this means that it is easy to add to patterns or combine them but very difficult to restructure them.* There are also the inherited patterns which are acquired ready made from other minds.

Because of this tendency to establish patterns and for

them to become ever more rigid one needs a means for disrupting the patterns in order to let the information come together in new ways. PO is that means as it is the tool of lateral thinking. PO is needed because of the behaviour of a self-maximizing memory system and PO works because of the nature of such a system. Within such a system some sort of pattern has to form. If the old pattern is sufficiently dislocated then a new pattern is formed and the process is insight restructuring.

PO is used to disrupt patterns. PO is used to dislocate patterns. PO is used as a catalyst to bring together information in a certain way. From that point on it is the natural behaviour of the mind that snaps the new pattern together. Without such behaviour PO would be useless.

The bigger the change from the old pattern the more likely is a new pattern to snap together. 'Reasonable' arrangements of information are too closely similar to the old arrangements to give new patterns. That is why PO works outside of reason. PO is concerned not with the reason for using information in a certain way but for the effect it will have. Once the new pattern has come about it must of course be judged in the usual way.

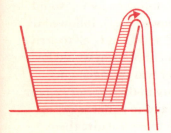

In emptying a bucket by a siphon the water must first be sucked upwards in the tube. This is an unnatural direction for water to travel. Once the water has reached a certain position then the siphon forms and the water will continue to flow naturally out of the bucket until it is empty. In the same way an unnatural use of information may be necessary to provoke a rearrangement that is itself perfectly natural.

Grammatical use of PO
PO can be used in any way that seems natural. The most important point is that anything covered by PO should

be clearly seen to be covered by PO. The two main functions of PO are first to protect an arrangement of information from judgment and to indicate that it is being used provocatively and second to challenge a particular arrangement of information such as an idea, a concept or a way of putting things. In the second case the material being challenged would be repeated and PO would be added to it. In the other case PO would cover new material.

1   PO as interjection

Here PO would be used by itself as a reply or even as an interruption much as NO is used. It would imply that a particular way of looking at things was being challenged.
e.g. 'The purpose of sport is to encourage the competitive spirit and the will to win.'
'Po!'

2   PO as preface

Here PO is used before a sentence or a phrase or a word that it is meant to qualify. The qualification may take the form of a challenge or it may take the form of introducing provocative material.
e.g. 'An organization can only function efficiently if all its members show absolute obedience.'
'Po function efficiently.'
or 'Po clockwork with the cogwheels made of rubber.'

3   PO as juxtaposition

When two words are going to be juxtaposed for no reason at all PO is used to indicate this relationship between them. This same use of PO is involved in the introduction of a random word into a discussion.
e.g. 'Travel po ink.'
or 'Po kangaroos.'

4   PO in the same positions as NO or NOT

PO can be used in any position in which NO or NOT could be used. In such a position PO would qualify exactly the same things as NO or NOT would qualify. e.g. 'Wednesday is po a holiday.'

In practice it is probably best to try to use PO always at the beginning of a sentence or phrase or right in front of the word to be qualified. PO does not have to be written in capital letters but until one is well used to it capital letters are preferable. If one is using PO and the other person does not understand its use then this can be most simply explained as follows:

1   Challenge function
PO means you may very well be right but let's try and look at it in another way.

2   Provocative function
PO means I am just saying that to see what it sets off in your mind, to see whether that way of putting things can stimulate any new ideas.

3   Antiarrogance function
PO means don't be so arrogant, so dogmatic. Don't have such a closed mind.

4   Overreaction
PO simply means, let's cool it. There is no point in getting upset about this.

Practice
PO is the language tool of lateral thinking. The concept and function of lateral thinking is crystallized in the use of PO. If one acquires skill in the use of PO then one has skill in the use of lateral thinking. For this reason practice in the use of PO is extremely important.
Learning how to use PO is similar to learning how to use NO. Learning how to use NO is however a gradual

process spread over many years. With PO one tries to achieve the same effect in a shorter time. It is much better to go slowly and carefully than to rush ahead and teach only a limited or even incorrect use of PO.

In teaching the use of PO it is far better to suggest the general concept of PO than to define rigidly the situations in which it can be used. Nevertheless one needs to show the practical use of PO in language and not just the theory behind it.

Since PO is the tool of lateral thinking any of the previous practice sessions could be reused with PO as the operative device. It is more useful however to devise special situations which indicate the function of PO more specifically.

In this section several aspects of the function of PO have been listed. These aspects can be mentioned in the course of explaining the nature of PO and as one mentions them one can give and ask for further examples. For the actual practice session it is better to group the functions of PO into a few broad uses than to confuse with the detail of each particular use.

The function of PO involves two basic aspects:
● The use of PO.
● The response to PO.

The response to PO
It is far better to learn the response to PO *before* the use of PO. The reason for this apparently paradoxical arrangement is that by learning how to respond to PO one actually learns the reason for using it. In addition by learning the response first one can then practise the use of PO in a more realistic way since it will not only be used but also responded to.

The points about the response to PO are as follows:

1   PO is never a judgment. This means that when PO is used to challenge something that you have said this does not imply disagreement or even doubt. PO is *never met* with a defence of what has been said. Nor is PO met with an exasperated, 'How else could it be put – how would *you* put it?' Furthermore PO is not an indication that the person saying it has a better alternative or even an alternative at all. What PO implies is, 'Without disagreeing with what you say let us – both of us – try and put things together in a different way. It is not me against you but a joint search for an alternative structuring.' It is important to stress this aspect of the *joint search*. It is important to stress that PO is not part of the antagonism of an argument. So one responds to PO by trying to generate alternatives *not* by irritation or by defending the original way of putting things.

2   PO may involve the provocative use of information. This means that information may be put together in a fantastic and completely unjustified way which is covered by PO. In responding to this use of PO one does not argue that the arrangement of information is unacceptable. One does not demand the reason for putting things together in this way. Nor does one sit back and imply, 'Very well if you want to put things like that you go ahead and show that it can be useful.' The provocative use of PO is to provide a stimulus which is to be used cooperatively by both parties. It implies: 'If we use this arrangement of information as a stimulus what can we both come up with?' So the response to the provocative use of PO is neither condemnation nor indifference but active cooperation.

3   PO may be used as a protection. This means that PO may be used to hold off judgment or to temporarily override a judgment that has resulted in a rejection. The response to this use of PO is *not to show that the judgment*

is necessary and should be applied at once. Nor is the response one of exasperation, 'If you won't accept the ordinary uses of right and wrong how can we ever proceed?' Nor is the response one of superior indifference, 'If you want to say that black is white and to play around with that idea for a while I shall just wait until you are through.' As before the proper response is a cooperative exploration of the new situation.

4   PO may be a relaxation. This means that when a situation has become tense through the development of rigid points of view and possibly overreactions, PO is suggested as a smile to relax the tension and to relax the rigid points of view. Here the only appropriate response is to respond with PO (with a mental shrug and a smile) and to relax the rigidity of the situation.

5   PO may be used ambiguously. There are times when it is not clear how PO is being used or what concept is being challenged. In such cases one simply asks for the person using PO either to be more specific or to agree that he really wants to use it in a general way.

In summary one may say that the most important aspect of the response to PO is to realize that it is not directed against anything but is a suggestion for cooperative attempts to restructure a situation. If one feels competitive then one can express this by using PO more effectively than the person suggesting it: that is to say one goes on to generate more alternatives than he does. PO may be an invitation to a race but never an invitation to a conflict.

The use of PO
For convenience the many uses of PO may be divided into three broad classes.

1   The generation of alternatives. Antiarrogance.

Relaxation. Reexamination of a concept. Rethinking. Restructuring. Indicating an awareness of the possibility of clichés or a rigid point of view.

2   Provocation. The use of arrangements of information as stimuli. Juxtapositions. Introduction of random words. Abolition of concept divisions. The use of fantasy and nonsense.

3   Protection and rescue. Holding off judgment. Temporarily reversing judgment. Removal of the NO label.

The generation of alternatives

PO is used to point out that a particular way of looking at a situation is only one view among many. PO is used to point out that a particular point of view appears to be held with an unjustified arrogance. The first level is merely to suggest that there may be other ways of looking at the situation. This is especially so when one uses PO as an antiarrogance device.

The next level is to invite restructuring of the situation. Here one asks for alternatives and goes on to supply them oneself.

PO may be applied to a whole idea, a whole sentence, a phrase, a concept or just a word.

Practice
1   The teacher asks a student (a particular student or a volunteer) to talk on some subject. The subject could be something like the following:
What is the use of space travel?
Should all medical aid be free?
Are straight roads better than winding ones?

In the course of the student's talk the teacher interrupts

with PO. The interruption repeats part of what the student has said and prefaces it with PO. The student is not expected to respond to PO at this stage. This is explained to him. He just pauses while the teacher interrupts and then carries on.

2　The teacher talks about a subject and this time the students are invited to interrupt with PO in the same way as the teacher had done in the preceding practice session. Subjects for discussion might include:
The usefulness of different languages.
Whether large organizations work better than small ones.
Was it easier to work alone or in a group?

Each time a student interrupts with PO the teacher responds by generating alternative ways of putting things and the students are encouraged to do the same. For example a discussion might go something like this:

TEACHER: Different languages are useful because they allow the development of different cultures and so provide more interest.
STUDENT: PO provide more interest.
TEACHER: Different cultures mean different ways of looking at life, different habits and ways of behaving, different art etc. All these are things one can learn about and find out about and compare to one's own. New patterns to be explored. Something to be done.
STUDENT: Different ways of expressing the same thing — they could be useful, they could be a waste of time.
TEACHER: Because of the different language communication is poor and so distinctness emerges instead of a general uniformity.
STUDENT: PO communication is poor.
TEACHER: People cannot talk easily to people with another language or read their books. People cannot influence each other so much.

STUDENT: People cannot influence each other. That may be a bad thing because from such interaction might come better understanding.

TEACHER: PO understanding.

STUDENT: They would know what the other person meant, what he was up to, what he wanted, what his values were.

3   It is quite likely that a discussion of this sort would very quickly become a two way discussion. If not then the teacher can deliberately arrange for a debate type discussion between two students. Each of them is allowed to use PO and so is the teacher who can interrupt with PO but is not allowed to take part in the discussion otherwise.

Comment

In this type of discussion it may become obvious that PO is being used mainly as a focusing device to indicate: 'explain what you mean by . . .' or, 'define that . . .' or, 'elaborate that point . . . .' If this seems to be the case then the teacher points out that the function of PO is to ask for a restructuring, to ask for *alternative* ways of putting things. When PO is next used the teacher calls for a pause and then invites the entire class to list different ways of putting whatever has been qualified by PO. For instance 'Po understanding' from the example given above might rise to the following:

Supposing that the other person reacts in the same way as you.

Things mean the same to the other person as to you.

Lessen the possibility of misunderstanding.

Full sympathy.

Communication without interpreters or intermediaries.

Ability to listen and respond.

None of these are complete or even very good definitions of 'understanding' but they are different ways of putting things. Perhaps the best of them is 'lessen the chance of misunderstanding'. This may seem a tautology but from an information point of view it says a great deal.

4 Picture interpretation. This is similar to the picture interpretation that was practised in an earlier session. The caption is removed from a photograph and a student (or students if there are enough copies of the photograph or other means for making it visible to all) is asked to interpret it. He offers an interpretation and then the teacher replies, 'Po'. This simply means, 'Very well. Go on. Generate another alternative. What else could it mean?'

This is a very simple use of PO but it is helpful to practise it since it indicates the use of PO in a much clearer manner than the other situations.

Provocation

This second use of PO simply indicates that the arrangement of information has no justification except the possibility that it might set off new lines of thought. Such an arrangement of information may be as fantastic or unreasonable as anyone can make it. The arrangement is not examined in itself but only in terms of what it sets off.

5 Juxtaposition. This is the simplest provocative arrangement of information. Two words are put together with PO inserted between them to indicate why they are put together. The pairs of words are then offered to the class one at a time. The session may be conducted in an open class with students volunteering suggestions which are listed by the teacher on a blackboard or else by some student who is asked to take notes. Alternatively the students can list their own ideas and these are collected and compared at the end.

Possible pairs of words might include:
Ice cream po electric light.
Horse po caterpillar.
Book po policeman.
Rain po Wednesday.
Stars po football.
Stars po decision.
Shoe po food.

The students are not specifically asked to relate the words, or to find some connection between the two or to show what the two words have in common. Any sort of ideas at all that arise are accepted. There is no question of directing the sort of ideas that the students ought to be having. If on reading through the results one cannot see the connection then one asks how it came about, one asks for the missing links. One does not care what the idea is but one does want to know how it came about.

6　Random word. This technique has been discussed in a previous chapter. It consists of introducing into the consideration of a subject a word which has no connection with the subject at all. The idea is to see what the random word triggers off. In this case PO would be used to introduce the random word. An alternative way of doing it would be to take some word which appeared to be vital in the discussion and couple it in juxtaposition with a random word by means of PO. Possible subjects for discussion might include:
Advantages of saving against spending.
Advantages of attack rather than defence in sport.
Knowing where to find information.
Why do fights start?
Should people do exactly what they want to?
The design of shoes.
Possible random words might include:
Fishing line.
Bus ticket.

Motor car horn.
Eggcup.

7   Concept reuniting. PO can be used to put together
again things that have been divided up into separate
concepts. PO can be used to remove labels and extract
information from pigeonholes. In order to put across
this function of PO one takes concepts which have been
created by a division (or which have created each other
by implication) and puts them together by means of PO.
Such paired concepts are presented to the class in the
same way as the juxtapositions were presented and the
ideas arising from this presentation are examined and
compared. In this instance it is better if the students
individually list their ideas so that when these are read
out at the end they can appreciate the usefulness of the
procedure.
Possible examples might include:
Soldiers po civilians.
Flexible po rigid.
Attacker po defender.
Order po chaos.
Liquid po solid.
Teacher po student.
Up po down.
Day po night.
North po south.
Right po wrong.
Male po female.

8   In addition to reacting to the juxtapositions and
paired concepts provided for them the students can be
asked to generate their own juxtapositions and paired
concepts. Suggestions for these are collected on slips of
paper and then a selection of these is fed back to the
students for their reaction. The simple exercise of
generating such juxtapositions and paired concepts *is
itself* very useful in making clear this particular use of
PO.

Protection and rescue

This function of PO is used to delay judgment. In effect it is used to delay rejection for that is the only sort of judgment which would remove an idea from consideration. PO may be used to protect an idea before it has been judged or it may be used to bring back into consideration an idea which has already been judged and rejected. In practice PO is attracted by the NO label. Whenever the NO label is used it is a direct indication of the current frame of reference against which every judgment must be made. By temporarily overriding the rejection with PO one is really reexamining the frame of reference itself.

9   A discussion is started between two students or between the teacher and a student. The discussion continues until either one or the other uses a NO rejection. At that point PO is used to overcome the rejection and the rejected statement is considered in itself to see what ideas it can trigger off.
Possible subjects for discussion might include:
Should people be encouraged to live in the country or in towns?
Does a welfare state encourage people to be lazy?
Is changing fashion in clothes a good thing?
How much should one do for oneself and how much should one pay other people to do for one?
Are classroom lessons too long?

A discussion might go something as follows:
TEACHER: People should be encouraged to live in the country because towns are not healthy.
STUDENT: Towns are not healthy. PO towns are healthy. Towns could be healthy with better planning and better traffic control. Perhaps towns could be more healthy mentally because of more social interaction.
TEACHER: Towns would have better health services because they would be more centralized and

communication would be better.

10   A subject is selected and the students are asked to think of all the negative things they can say about that subject. These are listed and then some of them are reexamined using PO. Quite obviously the number of negative things one can say about something is infinite. For instance about an apple one could say: 'It is not black. It is not purple. It is not mauve etc. It is not an orange. It is not a tomato etc.' In practice one would simply ignore that sort of list or pick out of it certain items. For instance 'An apple is not a tomato' could lead to the following idea: 'In some languages the word for tomato is derived from that for apple. In Italian a tomato is called a golden apple. In Sweden the word for an orange is derived from the word for an apple.' To avoid this sort of thing it is probably better to deal with abstract concepts or with functions rather than objects.

Possible subjects might include:
Work.
Freedom.
Duty.
Truth.
Obedience.
Boredom.

General comment on the use of PO
After the initial practice sessions in which the use of PO is obviously excessive and artificial one moves on to the more natural use of PO in ordinary discussion sessions. It is up to the teacher to use PO now and again to indicate how it should be used. The other important point is to watch how the students react to PO when it is used either by other students or by the teacher himself. An inappropriate reaction to PO indicates that the function of PO has not been understood. It is more important to emphasize the correct *reaction* to PO than

the correct *use* of it. Someone who knows how to react appropriately to PO will also know how to use it appropriately.

The one sided use of PO

PO is a device for use in one's own thinking and reacting as well as in communication with other people. In fact it is probably of more use in enabling one to use lateral thinking oneself than in allowing the use of lateral thinking in group discussions. This *private* use of PO obviously does not depend on other people understanding its function. In communication however it may come about that one person uses PO and the other person has no idea what it means. In that case one does not desist from using PO but explains what it means. Simple ways of explaining what PO means have been described earlier in this chapter. If in difficulty one could always say that it was a special form of 'suppose'.

Summary

PO is a language device with which to carry out lateral thinking. PO is an insight tool since it enables one to use information in a way that encourages escape from the established patterns and insight restructuring into new ones. PO performs a special function that it is impossible to perform adequately in language without PO. Other ways of carrying out this function are cumbersome, weak and ineffective. The more skill and practice one invests in the use of PO the more effective it becomes. It is not language that makes PO necessary but the mechanism of mind.